THE QUEEN OF SHEBA

THE WISEST WOMAN IN THE WORLD

The Queen of Sheba

The Wisest Woman in the World

Adapted by Princess M. Cullum Ph.D.

Illustrated by Suzi Eberhard

THE QUEEN OF SHEBA

THE WISEST WOMAN IN THE WORLD

Adapted by
Princess M. Cullum Ph.D.

Illustrated by Suzi Eberhard

For Samori, Samone, and Samaya
Because you are smart, intelligent, beautiful, and loved!
For B. Lemar, my husband, without whose love and support I could
never have completed this labor of love.

AuthorHouse™
1663 Liberty Drive
Bloomington, IN 47403
www.authorhouse.com
Phone: 1 (800) 839-8640

Scripture taken from the New King James Version.
Copyright ©1979,1980,1982
By Thomas Nelson, Inc. Used by permission. All rights reserved.
The Queen of Sheba The Wisest Woman in the World
Adapted by Princess M. Cullum
Illustrated by Suzi Eberhard

Published by AuthorHouse: 03/30/2016

Library of Congress Control Number: 2016904869

ISBN: 978-1-5049-8720-2 (sc)
ISBN: 978-1-5049-8721-9 (e)

Print information available on the last page.

This book is printed on acid-free paper.

authorHOUSE®

A Note to Parents from The Author:

As a mother, I am proud to tell the story of the Queen of Sheba. Ethiopian writers call her Makeda and claim her as their ancient Queen. She traveled over the hot desert and across the Red Sea to Jerusalem in search of wisdom, truth, and understanding.

The Bible sums up the importance of seeking wisdom in Matthew 12:42. The Queen of Sheba was superior to the generation Jesus wrestled with because she journeyed some 1200 miles to hear and see Solomon's wisdom and knowledge. Someone greater than Solomon was in their midst yet they would not listen to his God-given truths.

Let our generation and generations to come appreciate God's Word. We need to journey no further than the Bible for a deeper understanding of the true knowledge of the Lord.

"The queen of the South will rise up in the judgment with this generation and condemn it, for she came from the ends of the earth to hear the wisdom of Solomon; and indeed a greater than Solomon is here." – Matthew 12:42

The Queen of Sheba lived in Ethiopia long, long, ago. Ethiopia is a country in the continent of Africa. It has high mountains and a sparkling, blue river.

LORD, You have been our dwelling place in all generations. Before the mountains were brought forth, Or ever You had formed the earth and the world, Even from everlasting to everlasting, You are God. – Psalm 90:1-2

The Queen of Sheba had beautiful, dark skin the color of chocolate. Her eyes were the shape of almonds. Her black, braided hair hid under her golden crown covered with jewels and precious stones.

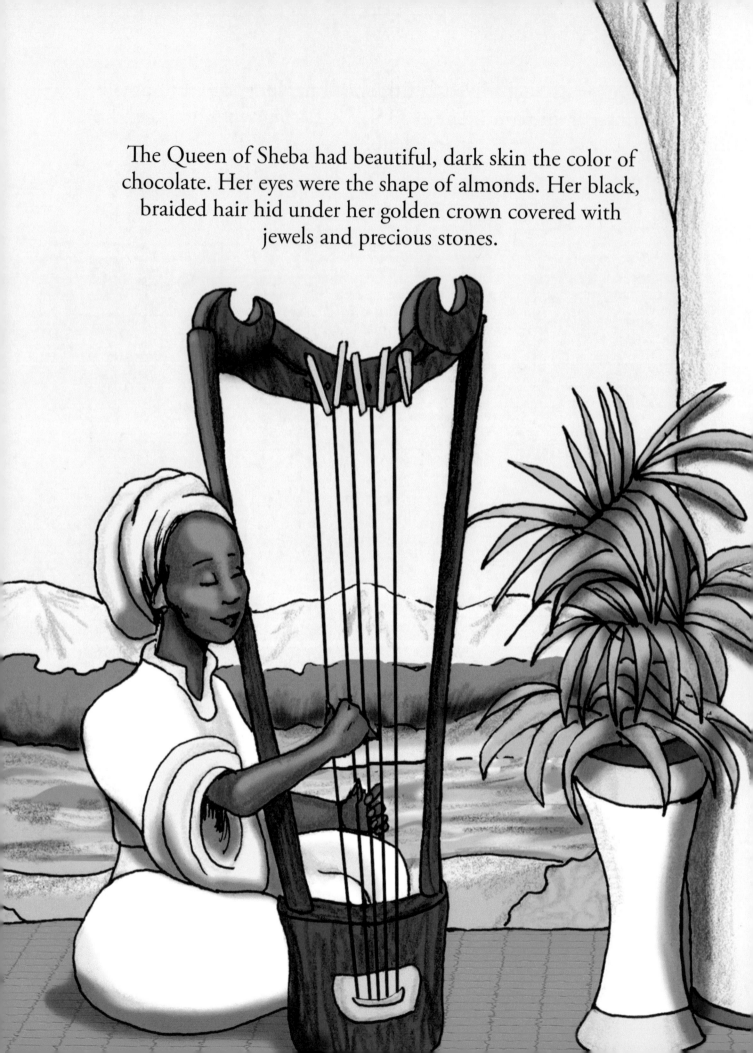

How much better to get wisdom than gold! And to get understanding is to be chosen rather than silver.
– Proverbs 16:16

The young queen was curious and liked solving riddles. She enjoyed going on adventures to exciting places to learn new things.

A wise man will hear and increase learning, And a man of understanding will attain wise counsel, To understand a proverb and an enigma, The words of the wise and their riddles. – Proverbs 1:5-6

"Therefore give to Your servant an understanding heart to judge Your people, that I may discern between good and evil. For who is able to judge this great people of Yours?"
– 1 Kings 3:9

One day, the queen heard a strange story about a rich, young king named Solomon in Jerusalem. Of all the gifts the king could ask God to give him, he asked for wisdom and knowledge.

The Queen of Sheba thought it was unusual for a king to ask for wisdom and knowledge. You can't see them, smell them, or even hear them. They must be special if King Solomon wished for them as his only gifts.

Then God said to Solomon: "Because this was in your heart, and you have not asked riches or wealth or honor or the life of your enemies, nor have you asked long life – but have asked wisdom and knowledge for yourself, that you may judge My people over whom I have made you king – wisdom and knowledge are granted to you; and I will give you riches and wealth and honor, such as none of the kings have had who were before you, nor shall any after you have the like." – 2 Chronicles 1:11-12

Mediterranean
Sea

Assyria

Israel

Palestine

Egypt

Arabia

Nile River

Red Sea

Ethiopia

The inquisitive queen knew she had to learn more about the mighty God who had given King Solomon this wisdom and knowledge. She began her long journey over the hot desert and across the Red Sea to test the king with hard questions.

Now when the queen of Sheba heard of the fame of Solomon concerning the name of the Lord, she came to test him with hard questions. – 1 Kings 10:1

Hidden behind a forest of almond, olive, and pine trees, Jerusalem was magnificent. The clever queen could hardly wait to meet King Solomon. Would he be able to solve her tricky riddles?

And men of all nations, from all the kings of the earth who had heard of his wisdom, came to hear the wisdom of Solomon. – 1 Kings 4:34

The Queen of Sheba gave King Solomon spices, gold, and precious stones. His round face and glowing skin reminded her of a sunrise.

She came to Jerusalem with a very great retinue, with camels that bore spices, and very much gold, and precious stones; and when she came to Solomon, she spoke with him about all that was in her heart.

– 1 Kings 10:2

The test came next. The Queen of Sheba saw many people who sought the king's wisdom and knowledge on who to marry, what crops to plant, and where to live.

"However I did not believe the words until I came and saw with my own eyes; and indeed the half was not told me. Your wisdom and prosperity exceed the fame of which I heard. Happy are your men and happy are these your servants, who stand continually before you and hear your wisdom!" – 1 Kings 10:7-8

Then, something *really* exciting happened. The Queen of Sheba witnessed King Solomon's judgments brought to light the blessing, prosperity, and joy of the Lord. His stories found a home in the queen's heart and changed her forever.

"Blessed be the Lord your God, who delighted in you, setting you on the throne of Israel! Because the Lord has loved Israel forever, therefore He made you king, to do justice and righteousness." – 1 King 10:9

Now King Solomon gave the queen of Sheba all she desired, whatever she asked, besides what Solomon had given her according to the royal generosity. So she turned and went to her own country, she and her servants. ~ 1 Kings 10:13

Adorned in a purple gown with a draping robe and long train, the Queen of Sheba went back to Ethiopia. She had learned exciting, new things from King Solomon about God. She was now the wisest woman in the world!

The Queen of Sheba traveled a long distance to meet the king who wanted wisdom and knowledge.

How far would you travel for wisdom and knowledge?

Begin by opening the Bible.

Questions

Before
the story:

1. How do we get wisdom and knowledge?
2. What is wisdom and where does it come from?
3. Name someone you think is wise and tell why.

During
the story:

1. Count how many times we read about wisdom and knowledge.
2. What country did the Queen of Sheba travel from?
3. Who did the Queen visit?

After
the story:

1. How far would you travel for wisdom and knowledge?
2. Where do you go to learn about God?
3. Name someone you talk with about God.

Activity

1. Tell where you would like to go, if you were an explorer.
2. Draw a picture of that place.
3. Write a sentence telling why you would like to go there.

Acknowledgments

This is a story about a curious girl who grows up to be a beautiful, wise, and knowledgeable woman. The Queen of Sheba reminds me of women I've known who have shaped the woman I am today. Throughout the writing, the people who kept me inspired were my beautiful mother, Bonnie Hampton, my mother-in-law, Ella Mae Cullum, Sally Patten, Liz Williams, Inga Walker, Ruth Ramsey, Earnestine Mason, Barbara Jones, Karen Blanchard, Gloria Mason, and Denise Billups. I could not have written this book without the encouragement of Jackie Hampton, Monique Johnson, and Melissa Johnson.

I created *The Queen of Sheba* as a way to share the Good News with my own daughters. I hope this story will one day find its way into the homes and hearts of children everywhere.

Printed in the United States
by Baker & Taylor Publisher Services